HELP!

Cries of the Heart

HELP!

Cries of the Heart

MONIQUE T. ROMER

Help! Cries of the Heart

Trilogy Christian Publishers
A Wholly Owned Subsidary of Trinity Broadcasting Network
2442 Michelle Drive, Tustin, CA 92780

10 9 8 7 6 5 4 3 2 1
Library of Congress Cataloging-in-Publication Data is available.

B-ISBN#: 979-8-89333-217-9
E-ISBN#: 979-8-89333-218-6

Dedication

I give all praise and honor to God, who is the author and the finisher of my faith, the lover of my soul, and the sustainer of my being. Without Him, I am nothing. Even in my imperfections, He shows me His love throughout His word and creation.

This book is dedicated also to my family, who has given me the greatest support. To my late mother, and to my father who have given me my foundation, you instilled in me Christian values and principles, and for that I say, thank you. You taught me how trusting in God's word and praying daily would sustain me throughout my life. You reminded us children, that our help cometh from the Lord and no matter where or what situation in life we find ourselves in, we are to be content, for our happiness is not found in wealth and riches, but in loving God and loving others. You taught us to learn to love and forgive.

Further, to my readers, listeners, and followers, I also dedicate this devotional to you. May God bless you, enrich you, transform you, and empower you through His Son Jesus Christ. For those who don't know Him, may these few words from this devotion open your eyes to see the wonderful Savior that He is. For those who know of His love and forgiveness, may these few words draw you even closer to His side.

In closing, always know that no matter what situation you find yourself in, God loves you. His forgiveness extends as far as the east is from the west. His arms are always open. Be blessed.

Acknowledgments

I would also like to acknowledge the ministries of The Annex Native Baptist Church and The Abundant Life Bible Church for not wavering in the gospel of Jesus Christ, you have both poured into me spiritually. Continue to stand on the principles of God's word being that light for believers and unbelievers in an ever-changing world.

> *Ye are the light of the world. A city that is set on an hill cannot be hid.*
>
> — Matthew 5:14 (KJV)

> *Not forsaking the assembling of ourselves together, as the manner of some is; but exhorting one another; and so much the more, as ye see the day approaching.*
>
> — Hebrews 10:25 (KJV)

To Pastor David Cartwright, Joan Shannell Evans, and Ryan Jones, thank you so much for taking this journey with me by walking by my side each step of the way and instructing me in the truth of God's word. Thank you also to Grant and Nicole Anderson, Sandra Badenhorst, and Timothy Miller for assisting me on my journey.

To Pastor Cranston, Pastor Gil, Pastor David Cartwright, and Pastor Anthony Rolle, thank you for allowing God to use you mightily to do the work He has sent you to do.

> *I must work the works of him that sent me, while it is day: the night cometh, when no man can work.*
>
> — John 9:4 (KJV)

Also through this work (the work of the gospel), He has been polishing, refining, and pruning me for His harvest that I may bear much fruit.

Foreword

Monique has a heart for the Lord and has seen Him do wonderful things in her life. She also has a concern for others, she senses their hurt and the pain that they may be experiencing and has come to the aid of many. She herself has experienced some difficulties in life, and we see that being expressed in her writing.

In her book, she talks about God's blessings, provision, and protection in the midst of life's adversities and how God brings beauty in the midst of it. The book is biblically rooted and provides practical steps we can follow.

I know Monique through the church where I am an Associate Pastor, and I have benefited from her counsel and help during the years.

I congratulate her on this, her first book, putting in print her thoughts and her heart's concern to help others along life's path.

— Pastor David Cartwright

Preface

On 16th November 2019, our world was struck with an unexplainable viral disease that was given the name COVID-19. It was nothing we had ever seen in our whole lives. "The first human cases in the world of the nasty disease were identified in Wuhan People's Republic of China, on or about 16th November 2019. The first human case in America was on the 21st January 2020. The World Health Organization declared the COVID-19 outbreak a Public Health Emergency of International Concern on 30th January 2020, and a pandemic on 11th March 2020."

Our world as we knew it up to that point had come to a stop. We were all so busy excelling in our spiritual lives, jobs, home, social media, technology, health, and commutation, we never saw it coming! Some pondered, *was it the hand of God moving upon the earth to capture our attention? Or have we forgotten the God of the universe, the God of our fathers, His promise, covenant, and commands that He requires of us? Or has God given us up to our reprobate minds?* Others may have asked this question, "Why would a loving God allow something like this to happen to innocent people like us or His children?"

During this time the world was locked down not only physically but also mentally. Relationships and friendships were tested, marriages failed, and families were broken apart. We were confronted with the truth of who we were, and about those we held near and dear. We saw deaths increase to unbelievable numbers, and people didn't know what to do to stop it. The devastation was great. Losing loved ones at the hands of COVID-19 left a scar that only God could heal, and many began to question Him. Our faith was tested, the church doors were closed, and learning how to deal with life situations and circumstances was difficult. Yes, people prayed. Prayers were going out all over the nations asking for God's intervention in the matter, but uncertainty loomed, and suicide among other things, was increasing.

In my mind however, I knew God was there with us no matter what we were facing, so in the midst of it all, I began to praise and exalt Him in all things, knowing that He does all things well.

However, I did struggle with some things, and one of the most troubling was the loss of souls, people dying without accepting Jesus Christ as their personal Savior, and that burden was the reason this book was birthed. It is still my burden today. We need to point the lost to Christ.

In this book, you will learn how we can receive everything God has for us. You may feel that there is no beauty in the ashes and that all hope is lost. For you, patience does not exist, you have forgotten all the blessings and provisions God has given. You no longer see the hand of God, and finding joy and peace has escaped out of the window, while greed and hate have crept in and amid adversity, you are wondering, "Where are you, God?"

Are we looking to others or scientists for an answer to our problem?

I realize that even though we look to others to solve our problems, it is true that "…God hath chosen the foolish things of the world to confound the wise, and God hath chosen the weak things of the world to confound the things which are mighty" (1 Corinthians 1:27, KJV).

God is in everything. That is the truth about God, He can meet you where you are. He can take your mess and turn it into a message to impact the lives of others.

Even though the pandemic is over, the world will never be the same as it was before, but we can stand on God's word that He does not change.

We all need to be reminded from time to time about the gospel of Jesus Christ. No matter what life throws our way, God always makes a way of escape. So don't be cheated out of what God has in store for you.

I have chosen to allow the Holy Spirit to lead and guide me along God's path, not just today but every day of my life, and to know that He is making all things new. As a believer in Jesus Christ, I want to express His love, character, grace, and compassion to the world. If each one reaches one, we can all be one in Him.

With this book, we get to experience and know the love of God and His love towards us, how to handle difficult times, and how to excel and proclaim the good news of the gospel to others, even your enemies. I am so grateful to be able to make this book available to you, and I hope you enjoy and embrace it as much as I do.

Be blessed.

Table of Contents

Introduction

Are you angry or uncertain about life's challenges and goals? Are you depressed, discouraged, struggling with the loss of a loved one, or have you received a bad medical report? Today is the day for a new start. You are about to learn that these life challenges are only stepping stones that lead to the path God has for your life. It's never too late. Life is not how it begins, but how it ends.

Before we begin a new start in life, we first must change our old mindset. Today you can decide to turn your negatives into positives, choose to forgive, speak life, and tell someone how much you love them. If we can take one step to look at ourselves in the mirror, we might see the change or changes we need to make.

Sometimes change is hard to make and even harder to accept, and people may be taken aback by who you are. Don't be discouraged by these obstacles but grow in maturity to a deeper level of faith.

This book will inspire you to search your heart, mind, body, and soul, giving you a wealth of knowledge and inspiration.

We all have dreams and aspirations that make us who we are; even if we choose to hide our imperfections, we must understand by revealing them, we can find our purpose.

Remember that you are unique. God's word says in Psalms 139:14, "I will praise thee: for I am fearfully and wonderfully made: marvelous are thy works; And my soul knoweth right well." (KJV) He reminds us in Luke 12:7, "But even the very hairs of your head are all numbered. Fear not therefore; ye are of more value than many sparrows." (KJV) God desires the best for His children. He promises to guide us toward making the right decisions. Regardless of what we encounter, God is faithful; His words will never change. When we rest in him, He will fight our battles, transform our hearts, and restore our lives.

SO LET THE JOURNEY BEGIN!!

My Heart's Desire and Purpose

Designed by Freepik

My life's goal is to show others how important it is to love, have childlike faith, walk in forgiveness, and let go of bitterness, hate, and anger. Simply, it is to live a life that allows God's holy word to work with the unique, extraordinary gifts and talents that He has given to us to use for Him.

It is an amazing truth that we were created by our heavenly Father and made in His likeness; we have His DNA living within us. Psalm 139:14 says, "I will praise thee; for I am fearfully and wonderfully made: Marvellous are thy works: And that my soul knoweth right well." (NKJV)

God has given us the ground of our lives to work and produce great things for His glory, but our most excellent harvest comes from what we plant in the garden of our soul, revealing our strengths and transforming our weaknesses.

Dream Big!

Listen to the Heart

Designed by Wayhomestudio Freepik

How often do we listen to our hearts? Are we afraid of what we will discover: insecurity, anger, lust, love, emptiness?

The Bible says in Jeremiah 17:9, "The heart is deceitful above all things, And desperately wicked; Who can know it?" (KJV)

Only God knows the heart of every man.

Proverbs 3:5 also says, "Trust in the LORD with all thine heart: And lean not unto thine own understanding. In all thy ways acknowledge him, And he shall direct thy paths." (KJV)

Proverbs 23:26 says, "My son, give me thine heart, And let thine eyes observe my ways." (KJV)

God wants the best for us, but more importantly, He knows what is best for us. He knows better than we do, how, left to ourselves, how easily our hearts can lead us astray, so He invites us to give their keeping to Him.

However, despite His invitation, we are often inclined to do our own thing. We are where we are because of our decisions. But God is faithful; He doesn't leave us alone to suffer. His love for us is unconditional, and all we have to do is ask, trust, wait, and obey. These four principles will lead us to peace with God. While applying these principles, we ought to, "Be still, and know that I am God: I will be exalted among the heathen, I will be exalted in the earth." (Psalm 46:10, KJV)

And while we are being still, there are some things we should consider.

- In our stillness, what do we hear?
- How often do we self-evaluate?
- Are we easily distracted?
- Are we listening to the opinions of others that don't justify the truth?
- Where and how do we spend our time?
- How do we see ourselves?
- Do we see ourselves as others do and not as God does?
- Who are we when no one is looking?
- Is it all a show?
- Or, if truth be told, do we act like we have it all together?
- Is there a void that needs fulfillment?

Listen to the Heart

After honestly answering these questions, let's find the courage and make a difference while transforming into a better version of ourselves.

Should we only react to circumstances when they become threatening? It is human nature to do just that, but we serve a forgiving God who allows us to realize our mistakes and offer forgiveness with sincerity. It is up to us to take responsibility for our faults to receive true forgiveness, healing, restoration, and divine enjoyment in life.

Ask these questions when seeking inner strength, truth, and guidance:

- Are we able to acknowledge that there is a problem?
- What are our motives?
- What are our intentions?
- Are we acting this out of selfishness or for self-praise?
- Is God pleased, and who gets the glory?
- Are we seeking sympathy from others or genuine help?

Are we truly willing to search our most intimate parts while submitting and seeking God's help?

Here are some steps to pursue:

- Surrender ourselves to God and give Him residency in our lives.
- Don't be afraid to let others help us.

- Allow our lives to matter while making the necessary changes. Don't live in the shadow of the dreams and failures of others.
- Discover your purpose and choose your destiny. Write it, read it, and run with it while speaking life.

From the beginning of time, God spoke everything into existence, and it was so. It was much more than words; it was life in its purest form.

How powerful are words?

Words spoken from the heart can encourage, motivate, strengthen, impact, and discourage not only our lives but also the lives of others.

It can be hard to discover who we are when pretending to be someone we're not. We need to allow ourselves to be free and embrace each passion with caution while being attentive to the heart.

How we choose to deal with our circumstances shapes our destiny. Will we leap forth as a mighty warrior or a whining wimp? The future is ours; walk into it.

The most influential book in history is called the Bible. This fantastic book unfolds God's mysteries that allow us to be more than conquerors and overcomers no matter what challenges we face. Genesis 1:27 says, "So God created man in his own image, in the image of God created he him: male and female created he them." (KJV) Knowing that He is our Father, we can cast all our cares on Him, for He cares for us. God desires a personal relationship with us in every way.

So let us lay aside all the weights that so easily beset us (our sins) while allowing God's Holy Spirit to transform our lives. If and when we fall short, remember forgiveness with sincerity is available to all. Joshua 1:9 reminds us, "Have not I commanded thee? Be strong and of a good courage; be not afraid, neither be thou dismayed: for the LORD thy God is with thee whithersoever thou goest." (KJV)

Keep going and keep growing, let's live a life beyond amazing.

My Life
Experience

Designed by Freepik

We don't get to live our lives without experiences, the things that happen to us. Some are good and some bad, but either way, they can affect who we are or become. The important thing is how we respond and the perspective we have as we go through them. When we remember, "And we know that all things work together for good to them that love God, to them who are the called according to his purpose." (Romans 8:28, KJV), it allows us to see God working in our lives and become better because of it. My experiences have been many, and I have seen the hand of God work tremendously in my life in each of these areas.

- *Beauty for ashes:* Through sincere repentance for sin, forgiveness, grace, and mercy are extended to all through Jesus Christ, as they were extended to me.
- *Faith in adversity:* In sickness, trials, uncertainty, and death, my faith was tested and strengthened through God's word.
- *God provides joy that conquers all:* There were times I allowed earthly possessions to substitute for happiness and contentment, but I have learnt the truth of the statement, "…the joy of the Lord is your strength" (Nehemiah 8:10, KJV).
- *Feeling peace in uncertain times:* When we decide to fight our battles in our own strength, fear replaces peace because we view the circum-stances in light of what we are able to do. In the midst of my battles, I learned to turn them over to God and allowed His peace to fill me and His power to consume them.
- *Mending broken hearts:* The heart is very delicate and very precious, and God's word tells us to "Keep your heart with all diligence," (Proverbs 4:23, NKJ) Freely trusting others without being careful with your heart can lead to wrong

My Life Experience

decisions, compromising situations, and a broken heart His word also says, however, that "The LORD is nigh unto them that are of a broken heart." (Psalm 34:18, KJV)

- *God gives joy that conquers all setbacks:* When others say I can't, God says, "You will."
- *God's love conquers fear and pain:* The love of God in our lives helps us to conquer fear and ease the pain that we experience, especially the pain that comes from being abused and misused in words, thoughts, and deeds. by those we care about
- *How to defuse anger:* Every day, we face verbal and physical abuse through words and actions. I have learned not to respond abruptly but to walk away and handle it with grace.
- *God's blessing, protection, and provision:* My life's decisions, changes, and choices were not always wise, but God kept me through them all.

It is indeed a privilege and pleasure to invite you into my world. Life is not easy, not with those that love you, or those that don't. I thank God for His incredible grace, mercy, and love throughout my life. Without Him, I don't know where I would be.

Through prayers, God has kept me. I am living and learning to call for help from my Heavenly Father whenever and wherever I need it. Some may say that God is not real, but I know that He is. I now know that everything in life is a choice and a chance. The choices we make in this life will undoubtedly create our destiny. Whether good or bad, all things work together for His glory.

We've been given one life to live on this side of heaven, something I have heard many say. What legacy are we leaving behind while impacting the lives of others around us? When we serve God with the right perspective, principle, and priority in life, our prayers, battles, and spiritual life will not only transform us but others around us.

When we have challenges and circumstances, can we count on family and friends to always be there for us like our heavenly Father will? He loves us unconditionally. A love that never fails even when we refuse it. God is the lover of my soul. He's always there, loving us each step of the way.

Creation speaks of His love every day. From the time the sun rises to light the day, until the moon shines at night, He gives air to breathe, and rivers that flow with fresh water to quench our thirst. The earth is the Lord's, and the fullness thereof. God gives it to us all. Songwriter, Dottie Rambo wrote, "If that isn't love, then the ocean is dry, there are no stars in the sky, and the little sparrow can't fly." God loves us through His creation.

Some may consider living for the now to be all there is. There is just one question. What happens in the afterlife? Where do we go? Or what awaits us? For believers, Jesus has answered that question for us in John 14:1-3. Have you decided on your final destination? While it's ok to live for the now, we must prepare for our final destination.

The only now we ought to live for, is to decide on what will be our final destination. "Behold, now is the accepted time; behold, now is the day of salvation". (2 Corinthians 6:2).

I live by faith. It's my daily decision, whether it's as simple as putting my trust in a chair or making the next step or something more meaningful as trusting God to wake me up in the morning. We all believe in something.

God has given us the opportunity for His Holy Spirit to live inside of us. We may experience His power, His word, His presence, also the ability to perform His will within the earth. Will we accept Him? For some, it will be yes, and for others, no. God will not demand us to take this gift but gives us free will to choose.

As human beings, we are weak and need God's intervention in our lives. During times of struggle, we call on God to assist us. We seek an immediate response even though our relationship is not right with Him. As His children, God wants us to know Him not only in times of despair but also in times of joy. He seeks an unconditional relationship.

When I think back over my life, two Bible characters come to mind: Moses and Joshua. God used both men in a mighty way to lead the children of Israel. They were God's voice to His people. I have come to learn that our most potent weapon in life is our mouth. At creation, God spoke everything into existence. Today, He still speaks to us through His holy spirit.

Just as God called Moses and Joshua to service, He is calling us to be strong and courageous. There was a time in my life when I made a wrong decision that I thought was right, but it wasn't, and it affected the lives of others I love so deeply. It is hard to see your wrong when you are not looking at it from a biblical perspective.

Life is not just about you, but it is living a life that first pleases God. Allow God's love to work through you so you can impact the lives of others. Everyone may not love you for it, but they will see in you the love of Christ.

When I'm in fear, I learn to trust God and be strong and courageous. Even though doubts arise, I cry out to Him in prayer, "All to thee I surrender, all to thee I freely give. Today I place it all in your hands. I receive Your peace and rest." During these times, His peace and love would overflow in my life.

I have experienced many challenges early on in my life. I decided to run away from home. I wanted to be free, and I didn't care how my parents felt. I was disobedient. It was short-lived when I soon realized that not everyone in life has your back. It was God's grace and mercy that saw me through and allowed me to overcome every obstacle.

My mother, now deceased, is still my inspiration. When I was young, I thought we would all live forever. Then I experienced death, a funeral, and unbearable pain. I thought, *How could this happen to me?*

I hid behind a façade, thinking I would escape the pain. I first had to realize that life can throw anything your way. I now live in hope and full assurance that my salvation is rooted and anchored in God. He is with me in the middle of my adversity, and He calms my storms.

His presence made me see that even when it doesn't work out the way we expect it to, He is still God. I am not a victim, but I am a victor.

He mends broken hearts, gives beauty for ashes, comforts, and shows compassion in the time of mourning. God blesses, and His love defuses anger. We are called and chosen with a purpose. By God's grace and His word, we can impact the world.

We can strive for perfection, but it will always elude us. We all have flaws but it's because of our flaws Jesus died.

You have nothing to lose today. Take a leap of faith, and watch God do the impossible. He is not looking for perfection, just a personal relationship with Him through salvation. Let's accept His salvation and rest in His assurance, allowing Him to fight for us.

Mending Broken Hearts

Designed by Freepik

What is a Broken Heart?

A broken heart may be brought on by a stressful situation, unnecessary extreme emotions, a feeling of rejection, a physical illness that leads to uncertainty, and many other causes. Before fixing a broken heart, let's see precisely what we are trying to mend or replace. Mending involves repairing something, thus renewing its usefulness and making it whole again. When something or someone is broken, we try to make them complete by encouraging them with hope not to feel damaged or left in despair. Our hearts are incredible muscular organs that pump blood through the circulatory system. We recognize it as the innermost part of our being, and therefore we associate that with the idea that we feel with our hearts.

When we experience various emotions, it affects our minds and ultimately affects us physically. It becomes even worse when our hearts ache from suffering emotionally. We have probably experienced some form of heartbreak during our lives, whether from our family members, friends, animals, death, or even from our spouse, the person we promised our hearts to. We all know how it feels. Perhaps to resolve the heartache, we develop negative thoughts or anger towards the person or relationship that has caused the damage.

Repairing a Broken Heart

Once the damage is caused, we toy with so many questions and feel confused at how broken and shattered we feel:

- How can a human being inflict this pain on another?
- Does anyone care?
- Will the pain ever go away?
- Why do I keep making the same mistake?
- Why do I allow someone else to hurt me?
- I will never give my heart to anyone again!
- Why am I stuck in this depressing state while they are out there having fun?

People will try and comfort you as if they know how you are feeling. Still, ultimately no one will ever understand the pain or your emotional connection to the specific situation. If people are trying to force you to escape your sadness, ask yourself the following questions to resolve your heavy heart at your own pace:

- What is your purpose?
- Why am I letting this hurtful situation have so much power over my life?
- Am I able to bare these feelings of hurt, brokenness, sadness, anger, and loneliness, knowing that they are a test to make me stronger?
- What is this situation trying to teach me?

Like an orchestra requires musicians to play different instruments to create beautiful music, you must acknowledge that your instrument is different from others but can still play the right tune. God is the conductor of our lives, and He has a plan to help us play beautiful music. He knows that we may not feel like playing or believe that we can play the right notes. There will be times when we might stray and play other music; however, God will guide us back only when we realize that we have to play it His way. In these situations, allow your faith to carry you through, and you will triumph over every situation. God loves it when your music is beautiful.

Guarding Your Heart

We ought to guard our hearts, not by blocking ourselves from all people but by praying for God's guidance in situations where direction is required. We call on Him, and He provides comfort and peace through Jesus Christ.

However, you are allowed to practice distancing yourself from the person or situation that has created the hurt. Respectfully, you have the freedom to feel what you feel and, after that, practice forgiveness. God's love will allow you to release any negative thoughts or feelings. Crying is not a sign of weakness but a form of release. So, if you must, shed those tears. There is no time limit on your healing process; only wise decision-making after that will help ensure the pain disappears. Seek support from those who have been through similar events; sharing stories often helps heal in a non-judgmental way. Also, your ability to help someone speaks to the fact that your healing process has begun.

Exploring God's Word
Toward Healing

The way the world looks at love is not heart and soul-based but of earthly material possessions. Despite our brokenness, God is always in the business of mending hearts, replacing a despised heart with a loving heart. "A broken and a contrite heart, O God, thou wilt not despise. (Psalms 51:17, KJV)

Regardless of what state you find yourself in, there is always a light at the end of the tunnel. "Cast all your cares upon Him; for He careth for you." (1 Peter 5:7, KJV)

Here are a few ways that God shows his compassion towards broken hearts. In this situation, consider the fact that although Jesus was sovereign, yet human, there were times when He endured heightened emotions with God's help:

- His compassion (feeding the 5000)
- His sadness (dealing with the death of Lazarus)
- His anger (when people were selling items in the temple)
- His joy (celebrating at the wedding feast)
- His brokenness (at Gethsemane)
- His healing (from the cross to His resurrection)
- His encouragement (teaching the word)
- His love and guidance for others (telling parables of the Good Samaritan or Prodigal Son)

There is nothing we can't do when we call on Jesus. He will never neglect us; He has experienced far worse situations. Moreover, He has been here since time began.

Bible references of God's promises:

- Jeremiah 29:11 — His plans are bigger than mine
- Philippians 4:6-7 — God has you covered in every situation; put your trust in Him. Pray with thankfulness about every concern
- Matthew 11:28-30 (KJV) — "Come unto me, all ye that labour and are heavy laden, and I will give you rest"

- Psalm 147:3 — Mending brokenness
- Isaiah 43:18 — Forget your past and allow God to deliver you and give you a future
- Revelation 21:4 — It will be worth it from beginning to end
- 2 Corinthians 4:8-10 — In your time of weakness, don't allow it to cripple you but to
- strengthen you
- Romans 8:28 — Through His providence God makes all things possible
- Psalm 34:18 — He comes alongside with compassion and brings relief
- Psalm 30:2-3 — God alone is a unique healer in brokenness

Never quit, and never count yourself out. Never let your past define you!

As beautiful as full-grown roses are, the process of pruning them can be tedious. Your growth will feel this way; however, it will be worth it in the end. Once you have healed, allow yourself to fly and be free. Remove the stronghold and begin to love again. Reclaim your independence also; live a little and laugh a lot. Make a list of all your strengths and accentuate them; you will start to notice that people will see them too, and you will attract the right people into your life.

God's love and compassion can mend any brokenness no matter how deep. He is closer than we realize or think and is willing and able to meet our needs if only we surrender, believe, and trust His promises. Always remember the battle is not ours but the Lord's. Stand still and see the salvation of the Lord. Remember also to help someone who is dealing with their heartbreak, even if you are not.

How to Love a Broken Person

Loving someone who is broken can require much patience. Remind them that we all experience hurt and that you love them regardless of their situation. Allow room for their healing and the forgiveness process, and appreciate them for who they are. Pray together and let them know that God loves them. In this new space, you will create fun memories that will pave a prosperous future ahead.

Pray for Healing

Father,

We know that You are our healer, and You do mend broken hearts. Help us to understand that only through forgiveness can we receive total healing.

May we be like You, strong in love and forgiveness. I surrender all.

I receive it in Jesus Christ, amen.

Now walk in wholeness, knowing you are completely loved today and forevermore. Do not let your past define you. With God's love, rise above and let your heart love again.

Rise

Lyrics Monique Romer & Ryan Jones

What do you see when you look deep within?

Is it all you've ever dreamed?
Are you on the path to fulfilling your destiny?
Are you living from day to day?
Are you concerned about what people say?
Why is it so easy staying down after a fall?
You've got to rise up and give it your all.

Nothing feels easy when you're all alone
Hope seems lost when your vision is blurred
So many times you've been counted out of the race.
Don't you worry about the arrows they throw
They may see scars but they'll never know
You have been chosen by God before time began
You have to rise up and answer His call.

You've got to rise above all odds
Rise above your storms
When every door seems closed
Put your faith in God

When you don't know what to do, He will see you
through.
He's waiting, He's waiting on you.

You'll never know how strong you can be
Just look within, there's hope to believe
Knowing that trials come to make you strong
Hold your head up, don't you cry
Weeping will only last for a night.
There is a breakthrough waiting in the morning light

Mending Broken Hearts

Live in the promise knowing He will provide.

You've got to rise above all odds
Rise above your storms
When every door seems closed
Put your faith in God
When you don't know what to do, He will see you
through.
He's waiting, He's waiting on you.

Repeat x 2

Keep on praying
Keep on praising

Keep on dancing
And until you see your breakthrough
Keep on singing
Keep on fighting
Keep on pushing
His favor is upon you
No more giving up
Nowhere to put your trust
Your God will lift you up
Your battles are already won
When you don't know what to do He's will see you
through
He's waiting, he's waiting on you.

Beauty
for Ashes

Designed by Freepik

Escaping a Life of Misery

Have you ever felt you were born into a life of misery with no way out? Some people feel that they've been taken advantage of, mistreated, bullied, or even dealt the wrong card in life. All through life, we've been labeled as ugly, overweight, skinny, dumb, and many more negative things. We've been made to feel underappreciated by those who say they love us.

If we only could see the beauty God sees in us, we wouldn't have to carry the burden of being accepted by society.

How can I see what God wants me to see? We can start by using the things that have been holding us back for years to our advantage. Turn the tables on how you see yourself because it doesn't matter what people think or speak of you, what matters is that you are created in God's image and likeness.

Therefore, you are beautiful!

Declare out loud, *"I am beautiful!"*

Defining Beauty

Beauty can be defined as the quality of being physically or spiritually attractive to someone or something; it is the quality or qualities in a person or thing that give pleasure to the sense of mind.

The problem lies in the world's definition of beauty, which restricts it to the physical appearance by society's standards. However, God's definition of beauty is having an inward peace of mind, a kind personality, a loving heart, a humble spirit, a forgiving soul, and loving someone like yourself.

The Bible's Definition of Beauty

There is a passage of Scripture that says, "Favor is deceitful, and beauty is vain: But a woman that feareth the LORD; she shall be praised. (Proverbs 31:30, KJV)

Being attractive should not be our ultimate desire; but to fear God. To fear God gives one a humble and gentle spirit far more desired by many, even above beauty. Here are Bible references that help us define beauty:

- *Deadly beauty:* Proverbs 6:20-29, Proverbs 23:27-28, Proverbs 29:3
- *Beauty is described as a flower, it is wonderful but it passes:* 1 Timothy 2:9, Psalm 103:15-16, Genesis 3:19, Job 19:25:29
- *Be wise as a serpent but harmless as a dove, for beauty is inward:* 1 Samuel 13:14 (David), Acts 13:22 (David), Job 1:1 (Job), Joshua 1 (Joshua), Exodus 3 4:10-12 (Moses)
- *Mary the Magnificent:* In Luke 1:46-55, Mary praises God in the beauty of holiness when she is told that she will be carrying the Messiah, Jesus Christ. Despite being troubled in her heart, Mary said to the angel, "Let it be to me according to your word." Mary found joy and beauty in her heart when visiting her relative Elizabeth, who was pregnant with John the Baptist. As she greets Elizabeth, the baby leaps for joy, and Mary is praised for her beautiful faith.
- *The Song of Miriam:* The Israelites, being in bondage for four hundred years, saw the magnificent hand of God deliver them out of the land of Egypt. They were mistreated and taken advantage of, and God heard their cries. God miraculously brought them out of Egypt, and they were victorious over their enemies. Moses said to the people, "And Moses said unto the people, Fear ye not, stand still, and see the salvation of the LORD, which he will shew to you

to day: for the Egyptians whom ye have seen to day, ye shall see them again no more for ever" (Exodus 14:13-14, KJV). God allowed them to see the defeat of their enemies, and they began to sing a song of praise expressing the beauty and the triumph of all God had done and would do for them, singing that the Lord shall reign forever and ever amen.

Beauty Rises from Ashes

Beauty from ashes reflects God's promise to the children of Israel that He had not forgotten them, and that His love for them is unwavering. He will see to it that their joy is restored. It reminds us that our lives are filled with trials, but God promises to restore us when we repent. He gives us beauty for ashes, joy for mourning, and the spirit of praise, for His glory.

Ash is a speck of dust or a powdery residue that remains after burning something. Ashes often remind us of death. It can also symbolize sorrow for our sins. The symbol of dust comes from Genesis, 3:19 "for dust you are, And to dust you shall return." Ashes were used for mourners or as a sign of repentance. They would place the dust on their foreheads as a sign of repentance for their sins or a lost loved one. Traditionally, some Christian faiths mourn the suffering endured by Jesus with the mark of ashes.

It also represents a willingness to repent of your sins and purify your soul in preparation for his return. In the Bible, God provides for those who grieve in Zion a restoration crown of beauty instead of ashes (Isaiah 61). Through Jesus' death, burial, and resurrection, we no longer have to cover ourselves in ashes for the repentance of our sins.

What manner of love is this that He loved us and sent His Son to be the propitiation for our sins! Jesus Christ is now our High Priest interceding on our behalf. Through His blood on the cross of Calvary, Jesus became our ultimate sacrifice, redeeming humanity which allows us to now have a more personal relationship with our Creator. If we say we have no sin, we are deceiving ourselves, and the truth is not in us. If we admit we are sinful by nature and confess our sins, He is faithful to instantly forgive us our sins, and to cleanse us from all unrighteousness. Through repentance, we can now receive salvation, forgiveness, the newness of life, love, and eternal life through His son Jesus Christ.

Today we see damaged and broken families. The good news is that Jesus came to build the Kingdom of God through the transformation of lives through repentance and forgiveness of sin. We can help rebuild our lives and society by showing others that there is hope, hope as in a new life in Jesus Christ.

Through Jesus' example on the cross, we each have something positive to offer to others. We owe a debt we can never repay. He paid a debt He did not owe, all because He loved us.

Dear Father,
    Help us to express our love and beauty to You and others every day.
    In Jesus' name, amen.

Faith in Adversity

Designed by Freepik

What Is Faith?

Faith is the complete trust and confidence in someone or something. A strong feeling of belief in one's religion. These are standard definitions for *faith*, but the Biblical definition is found in Hebrews 11:1. It says "...faith is the substance of things hoped for, the evidence of things not seen". Faith not only shows our character but by it, we recognize the many characteristics of God as we acknowledge His sovereign hand in every situation. Also, we exercise faith every day by getting out of bed, walking, driving, going to work, taking our next breath; the list can go on but these are the things we do without first thinking if we can.

What Is Adversity?

Adversity is described as a difficult and unpleasant situation, hardship, or challenge. It may be a physical, mental, social, emotional, or financial experience but is not limited to these challenges. God understands the level of adversity we can face and would not allow us to take on more than we can bear.

Finding Faith in Adversity

Many times, we see people come to faith in adversity and are sometimes amazed at how it happens. We can express our faith during difficult times by trusting in Jesus Christ to help us. Our faith provides us with an assurance that God will protect us, deliver us, or do whatever it is we need Him to do to bring us out.

Let's believe in God and remain faithful because we know that "God is not a man, that He should lie, neither the son of man that he should repent, hath he said, and shall he not do it? Or hath he spoken, and shall he not make it good?" (Numbers 23:19, KJV)

God promises, "I will never leave thee, nor forsake thee." (Hebrews 13:5, KJV) His arms are open wide; therefore, He will move mountains for you.

How to Overcome Adversity?

- *Accept* that you are facing challenges greater than what you can handle. This is when we realize that we need a divine intervention.
- *Acknowledge* any weakness or flaw in our character that the adversity brings to light.
- *Find that mother of progress,* the individual who will not judge you but will give wise counsel and support.
- *Build your character.* Once you understand who you are, seek to build in you the character that God wants through Scripture reading and prayer, and declare every day that you are a son/daughter of the Most High God.
- *Evaluate.* Look at what the adversity has taught you and how it has caused you to bloom. In the midst of it all, choose whether you would like to be victorious over the challenges you face, or remain static in pain.

You Have the Power to Overcome Adversity

Our challenges expose our weaknesses but can also help us not to make the same mistake twice.

They can highlight our strengths and desirable qualities that act as powerful weapons of change and resourceful creativity.

What are the types of adversities we face?

- Death of a loved one
- Loss of income
- Divorce
- Natural Disaster
- Illness
- Injury

Bible References to Help Us Face Adversity

We sometimes neglect the Bible when faced with adversity because we fail to recognize that it is a valuable resource filled with people who used their faith in God to conquer adversity.

- *Jesus:* Although perfect and the Son of God, Jesus was still human and experienced weaknesses. He relied on God's love to be the ultimate man of faith, expressing values of compassion, grace, and strength.
- *Joshua:* In Chapter 1 of Joshua, God says to Joshua three times, "Be strong and courageous; do not be frightened or dismayed, for the Lord your God is with you wherever you go." Again, in Deuteronomy 31:6, He tells Joshua to be strong and courageous. He was reinforcing the command so even if at first, we are frightened

and afraid, we should remember that Joshua also had to trust God and have faith.

- *Abraham:* Abraham had to sacrifice his son as a display of his faith.
- *Moses:* The redemption of the Israelites out of Egypt was not an easy task and required utmost strength and determination.
- *Noah:* Noah was divinely warned of bad things to come and trusted God enough to prepare an ark to save countless lives.
- *Daniel:* Daniel trusted God while surrounded by lions in the den, and he was delivered.

Process of Overcoming Adversity

Remind yourself to:

- Accept your conditions
- Avoid blaming others
- Practice patience
- Express yourself (via open communication)
- Control your anger
- Have a positive attitude towards solving your situation

Once you have overcome the adversity:

- Avoid repeating the same mistake by identifying the patterns

- Know that time heals all wounds
- Find the courage to face and conquer each situation
- Fill the emptiness with positive opportunities
- Learn to forgive
- Have a positive attitude
- Gain your independence back
- Begin a new chapter in your life

Starting a New Chapter of Life Without Adversity

Now that you are starting a new chapter in life free from adversity, be proactive in identifying situations that might lead you away from this freedom. Continue with faith and a grateful heart, knowing that you will rise above any new challenges.

You might have doubts and begin to question yourself. *Do I have what it takes to see myself through this? I can't take it any longer; why is this happening to me? Why is this happening now?* When answering these questions, be true to yourself; it is only in the truth that we can see clearly. When we dare to know our weaknesses and strengths, it allows us to ask God for specific guidance.

Faith allows us to *"Be still"* in adversity and know that He is God; He will be exalted among the nations, He will be exalted in the earth. (Psalm 46:10)

God's word is a promise to us that we can cast all of our cares on Him because He cares for us, and He wants us to enter a state of rest. This teaches us to believe in His promise and we will receive His intuitive truth, which gives us the ability to know or understand things without proof or evidence that it is a gift from God.

Your faith might be shaky right now, but here is a reminder to help you strengthen your belief. In Mark 9:14-29, there is a story of a father who brought his son to Jesus to be healed. The father admitted his imperfections which included doubt; however, he was desperate and pleaded with Jesus to help him. Because of his willingness to confess his weaknesses, God increased his faith, which reassured him of who he was trusting in.

In life, we need to take a step back and look at His creation in its entire splendor to see and know how BIG our God is and how our problems are easily solved through Him. Even if our circumstances don't work out the way we expect it, we can say that it is for His glory.

Songs of Faith

Often when I am faced with adversity and my faith starts to waiver, I go to a place that reminds me of how big my God is, whether it's through a song, His word, or a quiet place. It is a wonderful thing knowing that God knows your challenges before you realize what they are. He's waiting on you to lay them at His feet. I am assured that with God's grace, mercy, and love I can rest in Him knowing that my battles are won.

Prayer

Father,

Through Your word and spirit, empower us to be courageous in love, faith, honor, and trust as we follow the Lord Jesus Christ.

Amen

Feeling at Peace During Uncertain Times

Designed by DC Studio/Freepik

What Is Peace?

Peace is a state of freedom from anger, fear, conflict, and violence. In Hebrew, the word peace in the Bible, shalom, means total completeness, success, fulfillment, wholeness, harmony, security, and well-being.

Uncertain Times Challenge a Peaceful State of Being

Uncertainty or troubled times may cause sickness, confusion, displeasure, distress, worry, torment, misery, or grief. These emotions can display a lack of confidence in a person and consequently can affect one's physical or mental health.

The secret to peace is not in earthly possessions but in a personal relationship between man and a sovereign God. Jesus grants us a sense of peace that calms our souls and speaks to the very core of our uncertainties. So, in turbulent times, we should still give thanks.

When we are uncertain, we turn to the vices of this world for comfort. These vices give us a temporary or false perception of comfort. We neglect God and His word and pursue other means of fulfillment in our lives. As a result, we end up worse off than we were before.

We have allowed the world to dictate to us through social media platforms to entrap us. Sin goes against a peaceful state of mind. Discipline is a critical factor in finding peace in these uncertain times, so we ought to reach out to the one that gives "perfect peace", Jesus Christ.

The King of Peace

God's word promises us that we can have peace in these uncertain times. Matthew 7:7-8 (NKJV) says, "Ask, and it shall be given to you, seek, and you shall find, knock and it shall be opened unto you: For everyone that asks receives; and he that seeks finds; and to him that knocks it shall be opened." He is always available, but are you?

What an assurance to have that the King of Peace dealt with many trials and tribulations and still had the discipline to remain peaceful, even as He approached the cross. Let us be reminded that He is there holding our hand through the storm regardless of our situation.

Bible Verses

Let not your heart be troubled; you believe in God, believe also in Me.

— John 14:1 (NKJV)

Peace I leave with you, my peace I give unto you; not as the world giveth, give I unto you. Let not your heart be troubled neither let it be afraid.

— John 14:27 (KJV)

Therefore humble yourselves under the mighty hand of God, that He may exalt you in due time, casting all your care upon Him, for He cares for you.

— 1 Peter 5:6-7 (NKJV)

Be careful for nothing, but in everything by prayer and supplication, with thanksgiving, let your requests be made known to God; and the peace of God, which passeth all understanding, shall keep your hearts and minds through Christ Jesus."

— Philippians 4:6-7 (KJV)

Reflection of Bible Verses

So then, why does God allow trouble in the lives of His children? God allows hardship and suffering in the lives of His children for His glory and our good. In every situation and trying times, we begin to see our "Abba Father's" intimate hands. By relying on Him and acknowledging His sovereignty, our faith is strengthened, and we grow in love, trust, and humility. These attributes will then bring glory to His name.

It's not easy, but we have to be still to see the salvation of the Lord. Rest in His peace. In the Bible, we read about these strong men who relied on God during their most trying times, and God helped them through:

- Joseph — *sold into slavery*
- Moses — *leading the people of Israel out of Egypt into the Promised Land*
- David — *dealing with war and battles*
- Jeremiah — *the weeping prophet and the redemption of Israel*
- Paul — *Considered himself a prisoner of Christ and trusted God with his life*

Steps Toward Finding Peace

Ask yourself the following questions:

- Who am I?
- Where am I going?

- What do I want to accomplish in this place called life?
- Can I have peace in these uncertain and troubled times?
- How deeply would you like to achieve a state of peace?
- Do you have confidence that God is in control and will give you the peace you need in every situation?

Once you have truly reflected on these questions and answered each one, you will be one step closer to a peaceful state of being.

Confronting your problems is the first step to success. Now take the following steps to allow the peace of God to comfort and calm your soul:

- *Acknowledge who you are.* Are you willing to make the necessary change toward finding peace?
- *Write down each problem and place them into boxes.* Read out each problem to God, saying, "Father, I need Your help. I know you are a God of second chances, and I am willing to wait for my answers. I leave them in Your hands."
- *Remain prayerful, let go, and trust God.* You will already start to feel a sense of peace by handing over your problems to Him.
- *Surround yourself with positive and uplifting people*, people who highlight your strengths.

- *Release or express yourself when the need arises,* but do it calmly and in a rational manner in every situation.
- *Spend time getting to know yourself on all levels:* physically, mentally, and spiritually. Reflect on how you can improve in any of these areas to bring you peace.
- *If you find that these steps do not work for you, seek help from a counselor or pastor,* and remember that your state of mind affects those around you. Do it for you; if not for you, do it for those you love.

Final Prayer

Father,

We are so miserable at times we tend to forget who we are, where we come from, and that we belong to You. Help us to remember that in Christ, we are Your children — that we are known, loved, gifted, and cared for — now and forever.

Give us rest, calmness, and peace of mind to overcome every obstacle that comes our way.

We pray this in Jesus' name. Amen.

I Will Cast My Cares

Lyrics Monique Romer & Ryan Jones

I will cast my cares upon You
I will cast my cares upon You

For you've always seen me through
Lord you've been faithful, gracious
Your mercy always new
No one can ever love me like You do
I will cast my cares upon You.

When my heart is filled with grief
And my soul can find your peace
In the midst of my storms You were always there
I will cast my cares upon You

O Yes! He cares I know He cares
His heart is touch with my grief
When the days are weary and the long nights dreary
I know my Savior cares

I will cast my cares upon You
I will cast my cares upon You.

God's Blessings, Provision, and Protection

Designed by Freepik

L ife is full of distractions. It is so easy to lose our way, and if we are not careful, we can find ourselves separated from God and out of fellowship with Him. That is a lonely and unfruitful place to be.

God's ultimate desire is for His creation to have fellowship with Him, to be wholly His. When we go astray, He lovingly and patiently waits for us to return. Sometimes He gently speaks, not audibly as in Bible times but through a hymn or Scripture, or a well-placed word from someone He places in your path. If we don't hear, He gives us a little nudge, allowing things to happen in our lives to make us aware of our need for Him.

However He does it, God is good! Everything He does works out for our good and for the purpose of bringing us into fellowship with Him to worship Him and give Him glory. And He has every right to want our worship as He is the only one to whom worship and glory and honor is due.

> *...the four and twenty elders fall down before him that sat on the throne, and worship him that liveth for ever and ever, and cast their crowns before the throne, saying, Thou art worthy, O Lord, to receive glory and honor and power: for thou hast created all things, and for thy pleasure they are and were created.*

> — Revelations 4:10-11 (KJV)

Because God created all things for His purpose and all things belong to Him, He provides for and protects His children in every situation. When we trust in God and live for Him, Scripture says that we will be as tree planted by the waters, well-watered, protected from the heat, well-fed, and flourishing.

> *Blessed is the man that trusteth in the LORD, and whose hope the LORD is. For he shall be as a tree planted by the waters, and that spreadeth out her roots by the river, and shall not see when heat cometh, but her leaf shall be green; and shall not be careful in the year of drought, neither shall cease from yielding fruit.*

> — Jeremiah 17:7-8 (KJV)

But know that God does not show partiality. Jesus in His teachings on how we are to treat our enemies, says that we are to love them even as God loves them so that we can show ourselves as the children of God. Yes, God is just, and He will judge evil; evil cannot stand in His presence, and He chastises His children also when we do wrong, but He does it in love. Jesus says in Matthew 5:45 that the Father makes the sun to rise on the evil and the good, and He sends His rain on the just and the unjust. His love, grace, and compassion are extended to everyone and are new every morning. Great is His faithfulness!

Blessing

What is a blessing? A blessing is God's favor and protection over us. The hand of God works in our lives daily in beautiful ways, whether through good health, finances, relationships, or our very breath, but also in our tribulations. Sometimes we are made more aware of God and how He blesses us when we are faced with tribulations.

Abraham was a man whom God blessed, but He took him on a journey, and his faith was accounted unto him as righteousness. Three reasons why Abraham was blessed:

- *Abraham believed (Genesis 22:2-3, 9-10).* — Abraham demonstrated his faith in God through obedience. He was willing to sacrifice his son Isaac, believing that God who had given him the promise of his son was able to keep that promise. This was the ultimate test from God and God rewarded his faith.

- *Abraham was submissive (Genesis 22:2-3).*
  — Abraham obeyed God without question, argument, complaint, or conflict. He could have become emotional over God's instruction to sacrifice his son. He could have stalled for time, giving excuses so that he could keep Isaac with them a little longer. It is what we would have done, but he didn't. Abraham submitted to God's will, trusting His plan.
- *Abraham loved and worshipped God (Genesis 17:1-3).* — When God appeared to him and identified Himself and told Abraham to walk before Him and be perfect, Abraham fell on his face before God. His falling on face demonstrated his reverence for His God, a reverence that is born out of love.

All through Abraham's life, he'd seen and experienced God's faithfulness even when he made mistakes. Abraham, Jacob, Joseph, David, Moses, and Samuel, among others, were all men who were blessed, but their blessings did not come without pain or suffering. They trusted in God's plan and will for their lives, and they sought God's guidance, protection, and provision, leaving a beautiful testimony through their life story for us to follow.

Provision

Provision is the action of providing or supplying an unexpected need.

In God's word, we see that His provision of salvation was arranged before the creation of the universe (Ephesians 1:4). There are also stories in the Bible where we see God's provision of other needs:

- *Hagar and Ishmael (Genesis 21:16-17)* — Hagar cried, weeping for her child who was dying of thirst in the desert, but Scripture says God heard the voice of the lad. No matter whose voice God heard, the emphasis is on the fact that God provided for the need. God is concerned about everything that happens to us. He will make a way out of no way to show just how much He loves us. Yes, He will! A father will always provide for His children.
- *Jacob (Genesis 27:41-46, 28:1-5, 10-22)* — Even though Jacob was known as a trickster, God still provided for him. It doesn't matter how we start, but it does matter how we finish. God knows all things; He is omniscient. He cares and will always send help our way whether the need is great or small.
- *David (1 Samuel 24, 25, 26)* — After Samuel tells Saul that God has rejected him as king, Saul is troubled by an evil spirit sent from God. Jonathan, Saul's son, was David's soul mate. David was torn between two lovers (Saul, the king, who hated him, and Jonathan, whom he loved, his best friend). David always did what was right in God's sight, and God provided for

him in every possible way. From his defeating a lion to defeating Goliath, David was always committed to serving his God. Through dance and songs of praise, he rejoiced in his worship. God delights in the praises of His people. We ought to be committed like David to our Lord and continually worship Him as He shows us His hands of provision.

Protection

The action of protection is safeguarding or coverage over someone or something.

God promised to protect His people, keeping them safe. We all face giants. They come to steal, kill, and destroy. In His word, God promises to be our refuge and strong tower, a present help in times of trouble. In Psalm 91, we can find an intimate place of divine protection. This psalm lets us know that no threat can overcome God, and nothing catches Him by surprise.

God's protection is shown all through the Scriptures. One of my favorites is "God is our present help in times of trouble." (Psalm 46:1) He is always there. Everywhere. All the time. He is still protecting His people from the ever-present dangers and terrors which surround them.

In the midst of it all, God is faithful! Not just because He is God, but also when we're not faithful. When we put on the full armor of God, trust His word, have childlike faith, and apply these principles, we see the hand of God covering us.

One of the hardest things to do is find God's protection during a storm. Through it all, He gives us peace of mind that passes all understanding while trusting God no matter what happens. Speak to yourself and your circumstances and allow God's protection to comfort you.

Job, Nehemiah, Jeremiah, Hosea, John, Peter, Paul, Mary, and the woman with the issue of blood all proved God's willingness to keep His own. He promises to keep you and never leave you.

It plays an important role when seeking God's divine presence. "If my people, which are called by My name, shall humble themselves and pray and seek My face and turn from their wicked ways (repent, never do it again) then will I hear from heaven, and will forgive their sin, and will heal their land" (2 Chronicles 7:14.)

God's love, grace, mercy, blessings, provisions, and protection are always there for us. We need to tap in, submit, and receive it; the Father's arms are always open.

The one who is blessed is he who has learned to admire but not envy, follow not imitate, praise not flatter, lead not manipulate. Through submission, obedience, faith, and trust, in God, no matter what comes our way, our heavenly Father will always bless, provide, and protect His own.

Prayer

Father,

Today we submit ourselves and surrender all to You. We receive your divine blessing, protection, and provision for our lives, giving you all glory and honor that is due to You.

In the name of Jesus, Amen.

God's Love Conquers Fear and Pain

Designed by DC Studio/Freepik

What Is Love?

Love is a complex set of emotions, behaviors, and beliefs associated with strong feelings of affection, protectiveness, warmth, and respect for another person. It can also be an attraction that includes intimate desire felt by people who share a romantic relationship. There are four types of love:

- *Eros:* Erotic, passionate love
- *Pragma:* Enduring love that matures over many years, beautiful long-term relationship, for example, a couple. Commitment and dedication are required to reach this love.
- *Storge:* Love connection of parents for children, best friends
- *Agape:* God's love towards man

What Is Fear?

An unpleasant emotion is caused by a threat of danger, pain, or harm.

What Is Pain?

Pain is an uncomfortable feeling that tells you something may be wrong. It can be psychological, emotional, or physical.

There is a possibility that you can experience all of the above in just one moment. Let us examine what all three of these have in common.

Love itself creates an emotional roller coaster in our lives. Our fear of loving someone deeply is a result of the pain we assume we will endure if the relationship fails. We all dream at some point in our lives of a fairytale relationship. A fairy-tale relationship that wants all the wonderful emotions of love without the pain. When we experience emotional pain as a result of a failed relationship, it may leave us helpless, with-drawn, feeling unworthy, and with little reason to trust again. As a result, you may end up locking the door to your heart, never allowing anyone in again, a completely fragile state of being.

If we truly understand what it means to love with *agape* love, we can be free of all pain and fear. It's a love that's unconditional and requires one to put others above himself.

First, we must realize that we are made in the image of God. He loved us before we knew who we were. The Bible tells us of the greatest love story ever told. God sent His only son to die for our sins. God's love is the only love that never falters and never fails. Because we experience tragedy in our lives, we associate the pain of losing a loved one with how much God loves us. We would come to realize that even with agape love, we can experience pain and fear. We will never understand or comprehend the love the Father has for us.

Beloved, if God so loved us, we ought to love one another as stated in 1 John 4:7-11. Where love exists, fear and pain cannot exist. There is no fear in love because perfect love casts out all fear and torment. However, he who fears, has not been made perfect in love. We love Him because He first loved us. According to 1 John 4:18-19, we can rest in this assurance that He cares for us.

Fear is not of God. Fear is from the enemy. Satan came to kill, steal, and destroy. However, Jesus came that you may have life and have life more abundantly. Love doesn't take away but keeps on giving.

I believe we all can find comfort in knowing that we are not perfect and never will be perfect on this side of heaven. However, we can all strive towards perfection knowing there is someone always there to hold our hand and catch us when we fall. Despite our flaws and differences, He loves us through our pain.

From the beginning of time in the garden of creation, God called out to Adam in the cool of the day, "Where are you?" He replied,

> *"I heard your voice in the garden and I was afraid because I was naked and I hid myself."*
> *He then asked, "Who told you that you were naked? Have you eaten from the tree of which I commanded you not to eat?"*
> *Then the man said, "The woman whom you gave to be with me, she gave me of the tree, and I ate."*

— Genesis 3:9-12

Adam pitifully put the responsibility on God by not confessing his sin and taking full responsibility for his actions or any of the blame. This is how it is today with love when it doesn't work out due to circumstances such as financial struggles, late nights at work, lack of attention, and more. Providing love and affection slips through the cracks when priorities are ignored within the home such as spending quality time with family, celebrating special occasions, praying, and Bible study. When this happens, we find someone else to blame because it is easier to blame others for mistakes they did not commit, and we choose to deny confessing to a sin that we are ashamed of. It would have been easier to admit and face the consequences of their actions before this stage. Despite their sins, God's love covers them.

Love as a substitute sacrifice involves giving of oneself to another or the world without earthly gain. What happens to those who require earthly gain? When the earthly gain has faded away, is your love still strong when it is put to the test? Will you crash under pressure, or will you survive? We believe our lust for materialistic things will keep our loved ones and us happy. Some even put others at risk by stealing, robbing, and killing just to satisfy the lust of providing others with materialistic things. There is an immense amount of fear for the person committing these crimes, and perhaps even for the person receiving these goods. Is this love?

When we are apart from God, we are nothing and have no value. Although we are not perfect, we can receive unconditional love from God and then pass this on to others. Fill your void with the love of Jesus Christ, whose perfect love casts out all fears. Without fear pain dissolves. The love of God through His son Jesus, being the Substitute, is the ultimate Sacrifice of love.

> *For God so loved the world that He gave His only begotten Son, that whoever believes in Him should not perish but have everlasting life.*
>
> — John 3:16

As we learn to accept and receive His love, remember that He created us and will continue to sustain us. Even when we think the devil is having his way in our lives, understand that God is watching over us and would not allow anything to happen. He is caring, merciful, and loves without judgment. He will forever love us despite our flaws.

Words of advice from the Bible:

Keep your heart with all diligence, For out of it spring the issues of life. Put away from you a deceitful mouth, And put perverse lips far from you.

— Proverbs 4:23-25

The heart is deceitful above all things, And desperately wicked; Who can know it? I, the Lord, search the heart, I test the mind, Even to give every man according to his ways, According to the fruit of his doings.

— Jeremiah 17:9-10

Love is purity from the inside out flawless.

God Provides Joy that Conquers All Setbacks

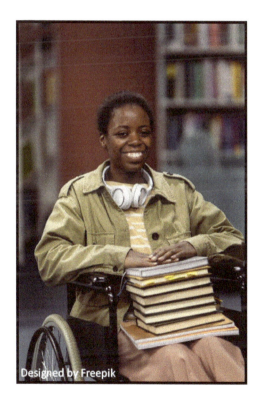

Designed by Freepik

It is challenging to respond positively when life situations are not understandable. Through these circumstances, we get to experience God's miraculous and gracious love that conquers all setbacks. Our God reigns, extending His tender loving care to all. The truth is that the God we serve can turn all things around, no matter how dire the circumstances may be. Let us take a closer look at one of the greatest gifts He offers to help us through the burdens we carry.

How Does Joy Provide Relief Through Suffering?

Joy is one of God's priceless treasures given to humanity. One may ask whether happiness and joy are both the same. How does one achieve this most priceless treasure during challenging times?

I am glad you asked.

Joy is an internal feeling of pleasure, contentment, peace, and rejoicing. Happiness is an external feeling that delights or makes us glad over a particular thing or event. That feeling possibly lasts for a moment or short term. We often think that they are both the same, and similar, and yet they are quite different. To be precise, they complement one another. Joy is an internal emotion that is not selfish or self-centered but creates an atmosphere of harmony, serenity, and contentment that uplifts others—giving such inner peace.

In a time of sorrow, regret, and sadness, one believes laughter and inner peace can calm the soul. Joy provides a prolonged boost of positivity and helps us and others get through difficult times. Happiness helps us delight in ourselves or someone else for only a moment.

One who desires happiness might say, "I would be happy if…"

- I could have it all
- Only I had a house, a car, kids, a spouse, a job, or entertainment
- Only I had more money and friends.

Ultimately, we know that self-gratification doesn't bring lasting happiness. Hence, the joy that God gives us through painful experiences is a spiritual one, but it can be felt physically through feelings of gratitude, forgiveness, and complete wholeness. This feeling expresses the purest form of love for ourselves and others.

Scripture Tells Us that After the Sorrow, Joy Will Follow

God offers us joy, love, and compassion even if we are enduring difficulties. Scripture tells us that Jesus feels our pain and has compassion:

Matthew 9:18 -26

Jehovah Rapha carries the story of Jarius' daughter and the woman with the issue of blood.

Jesus's compassion, love, and joy for His children are visible through the story of Jairus' daughter. Jairus shows extreme humility as an earthly father who only wants the best for his children no matter what the cost. Jairus had to put his faith in the healer called Jesus, as He was his only hope to save his daughter. When Jairus saw Jesus, he fell at His feet and begged Him earnestly, saying, "My daughter has just died, but come and lay your hand on her and she will live." So Jesus went with him, and a great multitude followed Him and thronged Him.

Along the path, a woman reached out to Jesus for her healing after bleeding for twelve years. Believing, she spoke words of faith, and she was immediately healed. It is amazing that while we are expecting our biggest miracle, life throws a curveball, and our faith starts to crumble. We then believe that our miracle will never happen. Jairus's daughter's healing might have been delayed, but it wasn't denied as Jesus did go to her and she was awakened from death.

Two miracles happened through Jesus' love and compassion, providing endless joy despite the delays. Our Father's love for us is eternal, and His compassion never fails.

John 11:20-35

Jehovah Rapha – Shammah –Lazarus' death.

The death of Lazarus touches the heart of our sovereign God. Jesus showed compassion and sensitivity while Mary and Martha were grieving over their brother Lazarus. We can only imagine how He must have felt when the news was told to Him. Jesus didn't immediately go to heal Lazarus. He knew that his sickness was not unto death, but for the glory of God, that the Son of God may be glorified through it.

One may ask, where is Jesus' compassion in this? Jesus had compassion and also felt their pain. By the time Jesus arrived at Bethany near Jerusalem, Lazarus was already dead for four days. Mary, Martha, and the Jewish community were all grieving his death. Martha said to Jesus, "Lord if You had been here, my brother would not have died" (John 11:20-27).

Jesus had a great love for Mary, Martha, and Lazarus. John 11:35 says that He wept when He was taken to Lazarus' grave, even knowing that He would raise Lazarus again. We may wonder also whether Jesus' tears were only sorrow over Lazarus' death (since it seemed He had tarried until Lazarus was dead), or were they also because of sorrow over the unbelief in the people that were there? Perhaps God wants to stretch our faith and broaden our love for Him through our burdens and sorrows. These difficulties prepare us for new levels of greatness for His glory. Jesus told Martha if she believed, she would see the glory of God; then they took away the stone and He called Lazarus and he came out of the grave. Imagine the joy of Mary and Martha.

Our relationship with God should bring about such inner peace and joy that is unspeakable and full of glory. Even through difficult times, we have that assurance of resting in His divine inner peace that surpasses all understanding. We can rest on God's promises, covenant, and full abundance of His compassion, forgiveness, grace, gratitude, and joy in every divine circumstance we may encounter.

Prayer

Dear Lord,

God of heaven and earth, O great and awesome God, how sovereign is your name. You keep Your covenant in Your word, and Your word is truth. Father, I accept Your unspeakable joy and Your abounding grace.

In Jesus' name, amen.

Speak Your Word Lord

Lyrics Monique Romer & Ryan Jones

Repeat x 2
Speak Your word, Lord.
Speak Your word, Lord.
Move by the power of Your Holy Ghost.
Speak Your word, Lord.
Speak Your word, Lord.
Because of Your love, I have been set free.

Move mightily, I pray.
Restore my Sight, that I may see You in Your glory.
Move mightily, I pray.
Restore my Joy, that I may praise and bless Your holy name.
Move mightily, I pray.
Cleanse and restore. Fill my life with Your presence; it's You I adore.
Move mightily, I pray.
I lift up my hands ever singing Your praises to the great I AM.

Speak Your word, Lord.
Speak Your word, Lord.
Move by the power of Your Holy Ghost.
Speak Your word, Lord.
Speak Your word, Lord.
Because of Your love I have been set free.

God Provides Joy that Conquers All Setbacks

Move mightily, I pray.
Through me today, 'cause You are the potter, and I am
the clay.
Move mightily, I pray.
So the world may see Your Holy Spirit living in me.

When You speak Your word, strongholds will fall.
There is nothing too big. You've conquered all.
I've hidden Your word inside my heart.
Your love for me shall not depart.

Speak Your word, Lord.
We need to hear from You, Lord.
Move by the power of Your Holy Ghost.
Speak Your word, Lord.
We need to hear from You, Lord.
We need to hear from You, Lord.
Because of Your love, I have been set free.

Greed as the Root of Sorrow

Designed by Freepik

Many factors could contribute to moments of great dissatisfaction, mourning, or sadness: straying away from God, death in the family, sickness, self-gratification, divorce, loss of earthly possessions (car, house, job, etc.), natural disasters (hurricane, earthquake, tsunami), financial loss, covetousness, or greed, but the one we will look at is greed.

"Thou shall not covet." is the most common translation of one of the Ten Commandments in the Bible. "You shall not covet your neighbor's house. You shall not covet your neighbor's wife, or his male or female servant, his ox or donkey, or anything that belongs to your neighbor."(Exodus 20:17)

This commandment, like others, focuses on thought, or man's heart. It is imperative not to set one's desire on things that are other people's possessions. One commandment specifically forbids the act of adultery.

Covetousness has been one of the leading factors that can cause great sorrow, especially when wanting what someone else has and not being content with what God has graciously given. Greed leads to envy and sprouts sorrow and grief. We need to look within and question why we measure our success according to the world's standards, while God's standard doesn't need materialism to bring us joy and contentment. We need to trust in God's plan and His provision for our lives.

As believers, we don't need to compare ourselves to others or yearn for what others have. That is a jealous spirit, and one that God hates. Comparison is an attitude of dissatisfaction with God's provision for our lives, which leads to an obsession with wanting more as noted by Robert Jeffress.

God has unique plans for our lives, so there's no need to compare ourselves or want to live our lives according to others' standards as this will not bring joy. His purpose for our lives is tailor-made; therefore, we must trust His sovereignty.

God has provided us with His assurance, covenant, and promise that He will never leave us nor forsake us, and He will always be here. Begin to pursue your purpose in life, and fill it with God's grace, promises, and His divine energy so you can soar like an eagle towards your destiny, one filled with continuous joy.

George W. Truett defined success as knowing the will of God and doing it. This sounds like the purest and most refined explanation of life, yet most of us lack this meaning and therefore live unsatisfied lives.

In Psalm 139, David expresses his awe that God knew him before he was conceived in his mother's womb.

How awesome is that! Even though we are given the choice of choosing, God in His sovereignty still watches over us and when we falter, He corrects our mess. God owes us nothing, yet His goodness and provision over in lives make all things possible.

In Robert Jeffress's book, *The Road Most Traveled*, he said contentment means 'being at peace with the unchangeable circumstances, choices, and even mistakes that shape my destiny.'

We must remind ourselves that everything we need God has placed in us. Say, "I will be satisfied with what God has given and put in me. I am designed for greatness."

Believe that He can. Speak these words every day and proclaim it and watch God take your mess and turn it into a message. Be blessed.

How to Defuse Anger While Embracing Patience

Designed by Freepik

Anger (wrath or rage) is one of twenty-one human emotions. It is an intense emotional state involving a strong, uncomfortable, and non-cooperative response to a perceived provocation, hurt, or threat.

When angered, we often act in ways outside of our godly character which can bring about anxiety, hatred, tension, frustration, etc. In life, we sometimes forget that evil exists in this fallen world, even with the best of us.

Different Types of Anger and Symptoms

- *Passive Anger* — Passive anger is expressed in different ways, it can be someone giving a cold shoulder, a fake smile, silent treatment, blaming others, or making excuses.
- *Aggressive Anger* — Aggressive anger is anger directed at another person to cause hurt physically, emotionally, or physiologically. It is displayed in bullying, yelling, putting others down (being amused by their failures), hitting, and other destructive behavior - destroying relationships and property, and selfishness.
- *Assertive Anger* — This is usually the best way to communicate feelings of anger because anger is expressed directly and in a non-threatening way to the person involved. A statement such as "I feel angry when you…" is an example. Communicating how you are feeling emotionally and trying to understand what others are feeling without causing distress or destruction.
- *Judgemental Anger* — Judgmental anger is usually a reaction to perceived injustice by someone else's shortcomings. The underlying factor is how we view ourselves, if we see

ourselves as either better than, or less than, others.

- *Self-Abusive* — Self-abusive anger is a feeling of hopelessness, unworthiness, humiliation, or shame. You might internalize those feelings every day and express them through anger — negative self-talk, self-harm, or an eating disorder.

Anger comes unbidden, no one decides to get angry, but we can control it and decide not to allow it to consume us or others around us. When we explode without control and infect others with anger, we might get an ego boost, but is it worth the damage to ourselves and others?

The Bible warns us about our anger. It tells us that we are not to rush to anger. James 1:19-20 says, "…let every man be swift to hear, slow to speak, slow to wrath; for the wrath of man does not produce the righteousness of God."

Also, Proverbs 14:29 says, "He who is slow to wrath has great understanding, But he who is impulsive exalts folly."

We see from Scripture that giving in to our anger is not good and not what God wants us to do. It points instead to us having a patient nature. Some may refer though to the Scripture in Matthew's gospel where Jesus made a whip and drove out those who were selling in the temple and overturned their money tables and their benches.

In short, He broke up their shop-keeping. Was He angry? Yes, He was. He had righteous indignation. This is a different kind of anger from those outlined above. It is being angry at the wrongdoing of others, and being motivated to do something to make the wrong right.

Jesus saw that the moneychangers had turned the use of the temple from a house of prayer into a market, and one that was defrauding the people. "And He said to them, It is written, My house shall be called a house of prayer; but you have made it a den of thieves." (Matthew 21:13.)

Jesus' action, however, does not free us to give in to our anger under the disguise of it being righteous indignation. That was Jesus, and He knew how to handle His anger. His life on earth was not characterized by His anger but instead by His love, compassion, and yes, patience. We are to follow His example and that of God. We read repeatedly in Scripture how God is slow to His anger.

> *The LORD is gracious and full of compassion, slow to anger and great in mercy.*
>
> — Psalm 145:8

> *The Lord is merciful and gracious, Slow to anger, and abounding in mercy.*
>
> — Psalm 103:8

> *And the LORD passed by before him, and proclaimed, The LORD, The LORD God, merciful and gracious, longsuffering, and abundant in goodness and truth.*
>
> — Exodus 34:6 (KJV)

It is our responsibility then to learn to control our anger. The best way to do that is to learn how to defuse it.

Ways to Defuse Your Temper:

- Think before speaking.
- Take a timeout. Release and let go.
- Calm down. Express yourself to the individual who has done you wrong with patience, love, and forgiveness.
- Unwind, exercise, listen to music, and enjoy the company of uplifting friends and loved ones.
- Don't hold grudges; it only allows negativity and bitterness to grow and take root.
- Use humor to release any tension or stress that may occur in your life and laugh a lot.
- Know when to ask for help. Each one of us needs to know that we have reliable people in our lives when we need to hear the truth but also when we need help.

What Is Patience?

The capacity to accept or tolerate delay, problems, or suffering without becoming annoyed or anxious.

To achieve harmony between patience and anger is often difficult. Sometimes we don't realize when we are angry until someone else acknowledges it. At this point, we have to find our way back to some sort of normalcy by exercising patience.

As we have looked at already, being patient is one of the ways we can diffuse anger. Do we have patience in these most trying times to diffuse our anger?

It is hard to be patient when you are going through difficulties. If you are not careful, anger and stress are two things that can ruin your life. Patience is essential to overcome frustrations and obstacles in everyday situations. It is a quality that brings happiness, paving the way to a healthy and peaceful life.

By analyzing our problem, it allows us to see the situation with clarity, truth, and love. In applying this principle, we can defuse and resolve our differences. This allows the peace of God to overflow in our lives. Some fight their battles as a means of survival, but God never intended for us to fight because His strength is perfect in our time of weakness. "If it is too big, it doesn't belong to you. We spend all of our time worrying instead of worshipping." (Steven Furtick).

It is the power of God that allows us to see His deliverance through our battles.

Ways A Person Can Practice Patience

Stop doing things that are not important to you but matter to others, especially when it frustrates you.

- Wait, think, and then approach a rational decision.
- Do not multitask. Deal with each task and thought one step at a time.

- Relax and take a deep breath, refocus, and then apply corrections to that which is important and true.

Shelter in God's grace and you will realize that the faithful one will not desert you when you are at the bottom! We can rest in God's purpose, plan, and understanding through prayers.

Patience is a virtue; embrace it, and treasure it! God is able.

Conclusion

What we've learned from this book so far is that we all make mistakes in life. These missteps show us who we are, and how vulnerable we can be when we allow others into our space and our hearts. Sometimes the good, the bad, and the ugly expose us for who we are. By all means, this is something good. The different characteristics remind us that we are mere humans and in need of a Savior, not just someone who can fill the void in our lives but someone who can meet us where we are.

While writing this book I have become even more aware of God's love for us. He gives us many talents and gifts to fulfill His will in our lives. However, we must be reminded that we must love Him first and above all. Secondly, we are to love our neighbors as ourselves. To fear God is the beginning of wisdom. We were all put here to fear God and keep His commandments. Because His grace and mercy are new every morning, we can come before Him daily in prayer, praise, and worship.

Everything we need is right inside of us; we just have to tap in and believe. Our different personalities don't come as a surprise to God. He knows our weaknesses and our faults. When we fall, He is faithful and just to forgive us. How great is His love! So amazing!

Life is full of surprises. I realized that we have to take both the good with the bad. We have learned that there will be days when we feel like giving up or giving in. We may face the death of a loved one, a broken heart, or a disappointing medical result. We have also learned that fully placing our trust in God gives us hope that is beyond this world's pain. Our faith in God prepares us for eternity.

Enjoy the journey, cry, laugh, love, be angry, embrace the hurt, and heal. Don't let this world defeat you. Christ lives within us and through Him, we are made perfect.

In conclusion, tap into the gift God has given you. Rest in the love of God and allow yourself to grow regardless of the challenges life throws your way. Don't be afraid to ask for help. Also, help others in need. God's design was that we all need each other to help us grow through life.

Love God; smile at life's storms. Live the life God intended you to have.

Have a blessed life in the Lord Jesus Christ and allow His Holy Spirit to guide you.

Author Bio

Monique Theresa Romer was born on the tranquil island of New Providence which comprises the lovely islands and cays of the Bahamas. She is the thirteenth of fifteen children. She graduated from H.O. Nash Senior High, (now Junior High) in 1993. Monique has worked in the service industry for many years. As a hotelier, she has learned many skills that didn't go without notice and have propelled her to various leadership positions.

Monique accepted the Lord as her personal Savior at the age of 18. Her desire to serve the Lord became the most important thing in her life. The need to see friends and loved ones come to faith in Jesus Christ has inspired her to share her faith through devotionals and songs. Monique loves to read and study her Bible. She understands that it is important for spiritual growth and keeping in the will of God. One of her favorite scriptures is Psalm 119: 9-11 "Wherewithal shall a young man cleanse his ways? By taking heed thereto according to thy word. With my whole heart have I sought thee: O let me not wander from thy commandments. Thy word have I hid in mine heart, that I might not sin against thee." To her, they are true words of wisdom.

The possibilities of Monique becoming a writer were far-fetched, but now she gives God thanks and praise for allowing her to share her heart with others in writing. When opportunities arise, she serves in ministry in her church through choirs, teen ministry and mission trips. She acknowledges The Annex Native Baptist Church and Abundant Life Bible Church as two churches that have been pillars in her life and have guided her on her Christian walk. She is also working on her new album that is soon to be released entitled "It All Belongs to You."

Presently, Monique is working as the Head of Housekeeping at Sandals Fowl Cay Resort, located in the picturesque Exuma Cays.

Bibliography

Dallas Theological Seminary. 2018. "Obey God and Leave the Consequences to Him — Charles Stanley." https://www.youtube.com/watch?v=kLuUvTyE8i8.

Elevation Church. n.d. "When The Battle Chooses You | Pastor Steven Furtick | Elevation Church." YouTube. https://www.youtube.com/watch?v=9yoaNVFo-tI.

First Baptist Dallas. 2020. "'Choosing Contentment Over Comparison' Dr. Robert Jeffress| July 19, 2020." https://www.youtube.com/watch?v=kYrXDCAxaYk.

Jeremiah, David. 2020. *Forward: Discovering God's Presence and Purpose in Your Tomorrow.* Thomas Nelson.

Printed in the USA
CPSIA information can be obtained
at www.ICGtesting.com
CBHW060615031224
18325CB00013B/139